Prai

Joël and I met at the bott

nent. He didn't get me to the top by just hoping I'd get there, he walked with me and told me what I might find out about myself on the way. He's done the same thing with this book. It's a book about courage and resolve and taking the next steps to live into the big life God made you for. This book is a cool cup of water on a long hike and is a story told by one of the most humble, loving guys I know. Buckle up. You're going to love the adventure.

—**Bob Goff,** *New York Times* best-selling author of *Love Does* and Hon. Consul for the Republic of Uganda

Since the beginning of time, God has called ordinary men and women to live extraordinary lives. Joël Malm walks among those who live life to the fullest, daring to follow God into the unknown, and becoming more Christlike along the way. This book provides a hands-on guide as to how to fulfill your purpose and passion. Prepare to live more courageously with each passing page.

—**Margaret Feinberg,** author of *Fight Back with Joy* and *Wonderstruck*

Have you ever had a dream that you didn't know what to do with? Have you ever hoped for something that seemed impossible? Most of us dream big dreams but we quickly shelve them, settling for the realities of real life. In his book *Vision Map,* Joël Malm gives us hope for our dreams . . . and not just hope but a practical process that moves your dream toward reality. With personal story, practical wisdom, and biblical support, Joël guides you in a journey to realizing the dream God has placed on your heart.

—**Jenni Catron,** church leader, author of *CLOUT: Discover and Unleash Your God-Given Influence*

Joël has taken his passion for leading real-world expeditions and applied it to helping us navigate our own God-given dreams.

—**Ben Arment,** author of *Dream Year*

Joël is a man of great character and passion for Jesus. The thing I love most about him is the way he was willing to think outside the box to implement God's unique calling on his life. The results have been nothing short of amazing!

—**John Bevere,** author, minister, Messenger International

If you've ever wanted to start something, if you've ever had a dream that you were sure the world needed, then this is the book that will get you going.

—**Jeff Goins,** author of *The Art of Work* and *Wrecked: When a Broken World Slams into Your Comfortable Life*

A simple, practical, powerful method for turning God-given dreams into reality.

—**James Scott Bell,** author and bestselling writing coach

I'm a dreamer. Always have been and always will be, but the greatest source of frustration in my life is bridging the gap between my dreams and reality. I've been waiting for someone to write a book like this that helps every dreamer see the next step before them. I am grateful the book finally exists, and if you are a dreamer, you will be too.

—**Chris Seay,** pastor of Ecclesia Houston

CHARTING A STEP-BY-STEP COURSE FOR
YOUR BIGGEST HOPES AND DREAMS

VISION MAP

Joël Malm

Pamela, Write that book!!

Moody Publishers
CHICAGO

Edited by: Jesse Lipes
Interior design: Ragont Design
Cover design: Studio Gearbox
Cover photo of mountain copyright © 2009 by jonmullen / iStock / 10802125. All rights reserved. Cover photo of typography copyright © by Yobro10 / Thinkstock / 120135996. All rights reserved.

Library of Congress Cataloging-in-Publication Data

Malm, Joël.
Vision map : charting a step-by-step course for your biggest hopes and dreams / by Joël Malm.
pages cm
ISBN 978-0-8024-1226-3
1. Dreams—Religious aspects—Christianity. 2. Success—Religious aspects—Christianity. 3. Goal (Psychology)--Religious aspects—Christianity. I. Title.
BR115.D74M35 2014
248.4—dc23

2014011021

We hope you enjoy this book from Moody Publishers. Our goal is to provide high-quality, thought-provoking books and products that connect truth to your real needs and challenges. For more information on other books and products written and produced from a biblical perspective, go to www.moodypublishers.com or write to:

Moody Publishers
820 N. LaSalle Boulevard
Chicago, IL 60610

1 3 5 7 9 10 8 6 4 2

Printed in the United States of America

To Emily, and my parents Rick and Jana Malm
who showed me a godly example of how to live boldly.

CONTENTS

FOREWORD

THE FIRST TIME I MET Joël Malm he made an offer I couldn't refuse:

"Do you want to hike the Inca Trail to Machu Picchu with me?"

How could I say no to that challenge?

I've been on several amazing adventures with him since that first offer. Every one of those trips has been a powerful experience. On every hike, the recurring theme is always take it one step at a time.

That's the message of the book you have in your hands.

I love the Vision Map concept because it focuses on going after the dream God gave you—step by step. Do what you can do, then pray and trust God to come through on the impossible.

If you've got a dream to start something new—a business, a ministry, or writing a book—then I think you will find this book invaluable. I can't think of a better person to walk you through the process of going after your dream than Joël Malm. He is a true entrepreneur and adventurer who has a heart to see you accomplish the great things God placed in your heart.

Mark Batterson
New York Times bestselling author of *The Circle Maker*

INTRODUCTION

THE CONVERSATION USUALLY goes one of two ways. I meet a new person and at some point they ask me: "So, where do you work?"

"Well . . . I lead outdoor expeditions with a spiritual focus."

At that moment the person either:

A) Smiles and says, "That's nice."

B) Lights up. A fire comes to their eyes, and I can see they are one of *those* people. If they are, the inevitable next question is, "How do you get into that line of work?"

I tell them I started the organization. The fire gets brighter and they immediately ask, "How do you start something like that?"

My usual answer is, "Well. Just start."

I realize that answer is unhelpful, and it may seem a bit cocky, but people rarely have time to hear me explain the circuitous, confusing, often frustrating, but fun-filled journey it's been getting to this point.

This book describes that journey. It's a response to the question, "How do you start something like that?"

It's for *those* people. *You* people. (More on that later.)

There are no overnight success stories. Let me repeat that. There are no overnight success stories.

I believe God wants to make the dream in your heart a reality—even if it seems far-fetched. You aren't crazy. You are a visionary.

I hope this book helps you navigate the waters of getting something started. I'll guide you through the process, step-by-step.

There's nothing more rewarding than watching God accomplish the goals He placed in your heart. I wish I could give you a simple answer for how to do this, but there isn't one. It requires time, hard work, and total dependence on Him.

There are no overnight success stories. Let me repeat that. There are no overnight success stories.

Every story is different. I'm convinced God does it that way on purpose. Otherwise we'd try to find a formula.

There is no formula. Let me repeat that too. There is no formula.

I've read tons of books by folks I would consider "outliers." Their stories are outside the bell curve of how things normally happen. They experience incredible, larger-than-life events. God has done truly unique things for them. Those stories are the exception. Most of us aren't going to fit into that outlier category. God will do miracles to bring your dream to pass, but in truth, I found the stories of outliers discouraging.

I've seen some pretty consistent things God uses to bring your dream to pass. I always found it encouraging to read the stories of how normal people like me got where they are today.

Here's my story and some of the important lessons I learned along the way. I hope you find it helpful.

1 } SO YOU'VE GOT AN IDEA?

IT ALL STARTED FOR ME ON a mountain in Russia. In a blizzard. At 16,000 feet. I could've written it off to oxygen deprivation, but something within me said it was more. God placed something big in my heart that day.

The blizzard pummeling our side of Mount Elbrus made our attempt to summit the highest peak in Europe an exercise in futility. We gave up for the day. Secretly, I was relieved. I realized earlier that morning when we pulled out the ice axes and roped our team together that I was in way over my head. This was above my climbing level; I had no experience ice climbing and only basic knowledge of how to use the axe in my hand. I was still loving it, but the situation made me remember there was some real danger involved.

On the way back down, we discovered that the blizzard was causing a whiteout that covered the trail markers. We stopped to reorient.

"Wait here. I find trail," my Ukrainian guide, Oksana, said in her flat Russian accent.

I nodded and knelt down in the deep snow. Ahead there was a break in the storm. Through the clouds I could see the Cheget Valley far below us—an encouraging sign.

I looked at my watch. It was noon. I thought of my family, soundly asleep back in Texas. They had no idea how dangerous conditions had become.

In that instant something hit me. It was one of those moments of transcendence. I felt alive and alert. I realized just how much I loved this kind of thing. I loved the thrill of climbing mountains. It was a spiritual experience for me, a way of deepening my sense of dependence on God and feeling connected to the sheer power of the vast world He created.

Travel experiences like this shaped my worldview. They gave me a wider perspective on life and a greater appreciation for God's amazing world—the people, the geography, the diversity.

I thought of my friends back in the US. They thought I was crazy when I announced I was planning to go climb a mountain in Russia. "Why would you do that? It's expensive isn't it?"

I tried hard to explain it, but they had no experience with mountain climbing, no frame of reference. I wished there was a way to show them how much they were missing. I thought of a favorite quote of mine from St. Augustine: "The world is a book and those who do not travel read only one page."

In that moment of transcendence, I realized something. I finally knew what I wanted to do with my life. I was on track to go to law school. That's what everyone said I'd be good at. I believed them, but I was never thrilled about the prospect.

In the midst of a blizzard hiding our way down the mountain, toward the safety of base camp, God placed a dream into my heart. He gave me a vision to start bringing people with me on these kinds of trips. I wanted to start helping others create spiritual adventures.

YOUR PROBLEM TO SOLVE

I'm convinced that God has given each of us a message to share with the world to bring Him glory. I'm also convinced that along with that message we all have a problem that God has uniquely equipped us to solve.

Let me establish something at the outset. God can solve any problem He wants to solve with the flit of an eyelash. He doesn't need us. For whatever reason, He chooses to let us participate in ultimate goal of bringing Himself glory. It's definitely not the most efficient method. I'm slow. I fumble the ball a lot. Inexplicably, God still chooses to use people like me. You are no exception. He wants to use you.

You may not have received a vision on a mountain in a blizzard. Your vision may have started by seeing a simple need. God works differently in each person. The circumstance surrounding how you got your God Idea isn't the important thing.

Doing it is.

Whether your goal is to write a book, go to college, pay off a huge debt, or start a business, never discount the dream God placed in your heart, however it may have come to you.

This book is about taking practical steps toward sharing your unique message and solving the problem God has equipped you to solve.

This book is for *those* people. Those who are certain God has given them a vision or dream. If you've got it, you know what I'm talking about. It's a burning desire to do something for God. It doesn't have to be clear, but there is something within you that yearns to solve some problem or share a unique message you think the world needs to hear.

How do you know if you are at that place?

Well, when you have a dream or vision that God has placed in your heart, you are obsessed with it. It's what you talk about *ad nauseam* with all your patient friends at the dinner table. You think about it all the time. Working on it feels like a moral imperative. Conversely, not doing it would feel almost sinful.

If you are at that place, I think you'll find this book helpful.

If you aren't there yet, I hope this book will inspire you. Read through it prayerfully. Then keep praying, explore, read lots of books, and start serving. God wants to show you His unique calling for your life.

If you had a dream that now seems impossible, or you wonder if your moment has passed, I want to encourage you. If you are still alive, then the dream is still alive—no matter how dead or impossible it may seem. I pray this book will revive the vision in your heart.

I've started quite a few things in my life. It hasn't always been easy. At times it can be downright hard. It often takes years.

In this book, I want to share the process I stumbled upon for taking a God Idea that seems so overwhelming that you don't know where to start, and breaking it down into smaller steps. I'll tell a little of my story along the way.

One warning: If you don't have a God Idea, this book might still help you, but you'll probably think some parts of it seem a little too hands-off.

You see, this book is for folks who have a dream and vision in their hearts that is so big it will be impossible to accomplish without God's direct intervention and miraculous provision. That's how I define a God Idea.

One of my main focuses is making sure God is always in the center of the mix. If yours isn't that kind of dream, you probably don't need this book.

So if you've got a dream—a really big, crazy vision that is impossible to accomplish without God—I think you might find this book helpful.

Enough set-up. God has a plan for us. We need to get moving!

"For we are his workmanship, created in Christ Jesus for good works, which God prepared beforehand, that we should walk in them."

—Ephesians 2:10

2 } GET A ONE-LINER

I MADE IT OFF THE MOUNTAIN and out of the Russian blizzard safely, but the fire that ignited in my heart was still burning. I started telling everyone about my idea. I was sure they'd all get excited about it too. Instead, I learned something crucial for every visionary.

I met with a prominent Christian leader to share my idea. I spent thirty minutes sharing my newfound life goal, my big God Idea.

The man listened attentively. I told him every angle. I shared everything I could think of that might get him excited about the idea. He seemed to like it. Then came the deathblow question.

"That's great. So what *exactly* are you doing?"

Grrr. *I just told you, dude!* I thought, as I smiled graciously. I walked away from that conversation learning an important lesson for anyone who has a vision: you need a clear, one-line explanation of what you are trying to accomplish.

It took me weeks to bumble my way through it. I had to seek

I walked away from that conversation learning an important lesson for anyone who has a vision: you need a clear, one-line explanation of what you are trying to accomplish.

lots of counsel and share the idea with many people who gave me confused looks. But I finally came up with a simple, one-line explanation. The next time someone asked me what I was trying to do I had it down cold: "I want to take people on spiritually focused adventure trips around the world."

The best way to refine a one-liner is to say it over and over and over. Talk it out. Watch how people respond. Tap into elements that seem to consistently bring out the "wow" response in people as they listen. Narrow the vision down to the clearest possible explanation.

I've heard it said, "If it's a mist in your head, it will be a fog in the listener's head." It's true. You need a clear, concise explanation of what you are trying to accomplish. It can't be foggy.

I realized, after lots of talking it through, that my ultimate goal was to use travel to give people a bigger perspective on their lives. That was my problem to solve. Make sure you are very specific. Tell people what problem your vision is going to solve. You'll refine it in the process.

Many people share their one-liners with me. I recently heard one that sounded something like this: *Create strategic alliances that empower synergistic approaches to complex problem solving.*

I read it a few times trying to figure it out. I didn't want to discourage him, but I had to be honest. "That sounds amazing!

Lots of fancy, hip words. But what the heck does it mean? What are you trying to do?"

When I asked him some clarifying questions and we got down to the nuts and bolts it became clear that he still didn't know *exactly* what he was trying to do. His one-liner had some glamour, but if no one can understand his ultimate goal, it isn't serving its purpose.

I know lots of missionaries who send me newsletters about their work. I'm confident they are doing something of value because I know them. However, even though I support them, I still have no idea what they do. Even when I directly ask them I can't get a clear statement of their main focus. Some have shared that they're struggling to raise funds for very good projects. I wonder if part of their challenge is that they haven't taken the time to define their vision. If you can develop a clear picture, others will get on board. We follow clear visions.

When God gives you a dream or a problem to solve, it usually first appears in a general, overarching idea with very few specifics. You see a problem and want to solve it. I only knew I wanted to help people have experiences that expanded their perspective. It wasn't super clear.

I don't think anyone ever gets a vision for something amazing with all the details exactly laid out. It takes time. It takes talking it out. It takes homing in on exactly what you want to accomplish.

Don't be afraid if your one-liner sounds too big or even impossible. William Wilberforce, the man who is considered to be largely responsible for ending the slave trade in most of the British Empire, had a huge vision. On October 28, 1787, he wrote out his one-liner:

"God Almighty has set before me two great objects: the suppression of the slave trade and the reformation of morals."[1]

Seriously, Will? Think about this. That was a huge dream. Slavery was so prevalent in his time that I'm certain this goal seemed absolutely impossible, bordering on ridiculous. It would be like saying, "I'm going to eliminate cigarette smoking!"

Guess what? It took forty-six years, but it happened. Wilberforce saw slavery abolished in almost the entirety of the British Empire three days before he went to be with the Lord for eternity. He worked his entire life on that dream.

A single mother I shared this concept with developed this one-liner:

Raise kids who love Jesus and people.

Have you seen this world we live in? Talk about an impossible dream! But God placed that vision in her heart, and she is pursuing it with all she's got.

I don't think there's anything wrong with having a one-liner for every area of your life. In fact, I'll be bold and say I think you *need* one for every area of your life. I have the guys in my Summit Life Coaching Program write one for family, finances, career, and ministry. It's amazing to see what happens when people write out clear visions for their lives.

God wants to give you a vision for every area of your life.

Like we discussed, developing a one-liner isn't necessarily easy. It will take some time, some thought, and probably a few bumbled attempts at explaining it to people. Don't get discouraged if you are at this phase of the process right now. It will get clearer. As you keep explaining and exploring the problem you want to solve, you will eventually get to a place where you can clearly articulate what you are trying to accomplish.

Once you've got the one-liner, run it past a few folks. See how they respond. Do they understand it? If not, you may need to keep honing it. There is a problem that God has placed you on this earth to solve. You have a unique message to share with the world that will bring God glory.

Pretty confident you've got a good, clear one-liner? Then write it down.

ON THE WALL

An African friend visiting the US pointed out how strange he thought it was that hospitals have a vision statement on the wall.

"Doesn't everyone know what a hospital is there to do?"

It's kind of funny when you think about it, but the fact is we all have a tendency to forget. I get into a routine and forget why I'm doing what I'm doing all the time. That's why it's so important to write out your one-line vision.

"Write the vision; make it plain on tablets, so he may run who reads it" (Habakkuk 2:2).

I think the best possible thing you can do is to write your one-liner out in a visible place. Make it large.

When I finally had my one-liner, I ran to the store and picked up a black marker and large poster board. This was the beginning of a process I stumbled upon that has helped me navigate my way through many projects and visions God has given me over the years.

I CALL IT A VISION MAP

The concept isn't complicated. But it really helps me clarify my vision.

Some people spend thousands of dollars on consultants, displays, and spreadsheets to explain their goal. Not me. No, I was a poor college student. I spent a few bucks, but it served the purpose. I stuck the poster board up on the wall of my bedroom. This was how my Vision Map began.

At the top I wrote out my one-liner in big black letters:

Take people on spiritually focused adventure trips around the world.

The vision greeted me every morning now. It was in front of me. It was clear. I had a tangible, one-line goal to run with.

Several people helped me nail it down. You'll probably need someone to help you do the same. I discovered early on that if I was going to pull off this dream God placed in my heart, I needed some trusted advisors. You will too.

> *Clarity is the most important thing. I can compare clarity to pruning in gardening. If you are not clear, nothing is going to happen. You have to be clear. Then you have to be confident about your vision. And after that, you just have to put a lot of work in.*
>
> —Diane von Furstenberg, Fashion Designer

3} FIND ADVISORS

TAKE A MOMENT RIGHT NOW to memorize this verse: *"Without counsel plans fail, but with many advisors they succeed"* (Prov. 15:22). Say it a few times to yourself. It's one of the most important principles anyone with a wild idea can ever learn. You need advisors.

When I came back from Russia, all fired up with my wild idea, I ran it past my most trusted advisor: my dad. I told him what I wanted to do. I still wasn't clear what it would look like, but I did my best to explain what I was trying to accomplish.

He loved the idea. Then he did what the best advisors do. He asked questions.

BLIP, BLIP, BLIP

In 1886, Heinrich Hertz discovered that radio waves could be bounced off of solid objects. During World War II, this discovery was developed into something called Radio Detection and Ranging, a.k.a. *RADAR*.

Radar sends off electromagnetic waves and waits for the waves to bounce off a solid object. When the solid object reflects the signal back in the form of a "blip," the receiver is able to get a feel for what's ahead.

May I suggest that a good advisor should serve like radar?

The best advisors won't tell you what to do—that is God's job. Instead, they are simply solid objects that serve as sounding boards, reflecting back valuable insight that will help you navigate uncertain terrain.

When a dream is placed in your heart, priority number one should be to seek out advisors. Good ones. Solid folks you can bounce ideas off.

When I'm confused or overwhelmed, I usually prefer to have my pastor or advisor tell me what to do. That makes it easy. A good advisor directs you to the Lord. Also, a good advisor will ask questions. They'll point out blind spots and give suggestions to help you navigate tricky challenges.

My dad and a few other guys helped me with that. They asked me questions I hadn't considered. They pointed out potential problems. I'm certain that I avoided a lot of rookie mistakes when I was getting started simply by seeking out counsel.

I did my own fair share of asking questions too. Every time I met with advisors I always came with a list of questions I wrote out beforehand.

I asked questions like:

Have you ever heard of anyone doing anything like what I just proposed?

What are some lessons you learned the hard way?

What steps would you recommend I take at this point?

What books should I be reading?

Do you know anyone I should know that can help me navigate this?

It might be challenging if your vision is something completely new. How do you find guys to help you navigate those waters? It's easier than you'd think, mostly because God's principles work in every situation.

Make sure you find an advisor who will share principles they've learned. Look for someone who is walking their talk—someone who has shown a radical commitment to Christ and who is more concerned about what He is doing in you than about your comfort. You need bold folks who tell you the truth, not what they think you want to hear.

I love this old African proverb: "Never buy clothes from a naked man."

Here's my translation: Don't take advice from someone who clearly hasn't shown themselves knowledgeable in that area.

If you are going to start a business, find someone who has run a similar business. It doesn't have to be identical to yours, but find someone who has clearly been successful in a similar endeavor while using God's principles.

If possible, find someone who did it right the first time. Latch on to guys like that and pump them for wisdom. They will be invaluable resources as you seek God and set out to implement your God Idea.

I've heard it said that the only things that will change you are the people you meet and the books you read. Some of your best advisors may not necessarily be in person. Some of your best input may come through reading books.

The first thing I started doing once I had my clear one-line vision statement was read. I read everything I could get my hands on—leadership books, travel books, boring books about organizational structure. I read anything that I thought would help me gain knowledge I might need.

Some of the most powerful lessons I've ever learned came from books. Count on the wisdom of those who have gone before you and taken the time to write down their experiences and insights. Reading is a way to get access to advisors you may never be able to meet face-to-face.

I believe visionaries need to become avid readers. You need to read. A lot. Leaders are readers.

I believe visionaries need to become avid readers. You need to read. A lot. Leaders are readers.

Be prepared. There will be some advisors who won't be very encouraging. There were times when I walked away from a conversation with an advisor feeling profoundly discouraged. One guy I visited was delighted to point out every possible weak point in my plan. He told me all the disastrous things that could happen. He reminded me I had no experience doing this. I left feeling hopeless. There are some advisors who have that effect.

Fortunately, a friend of mine was with me in that meeting. He could sense I was discouraged. He stopped me in the hall as we were leaving the building and said something I'll never forget:

"Well, he sure pointed out lots of things that could go wrong.

But don't forget, he's just a guy in an office. You are the one with the vision and the courage to do this."

His words lifted my spirits. It reminded me—listen to advisors, but don't let them discourage you.

As the old saying goes, "Eat the fish and spit out the bones." What he was saying was important for me to hear, but just because he was saying it didn't mean every disastrous thing he mentioned was inevitable. I needed to be alert to danger, but I shouldn't let a discouraging word keep me from pursuing what God put in my heart.

Some of your worst naysayers could end up being your best advisors, if you handle the criticism correctly. Don't let them get you down.

Once you've received counsel, it's time to start charting a course. Time to make a plan. It's time to start taking steps toward your dream. If your dream is a big one, it will probably seem overwhelming. You may not even know where to start.

Enter the Vision Map.

". . . in an abundance of counselors there is safety."

—Proverbs 11:14

4 } DRAW A MAP

I WAS JUST ABOUT TO graduate from college. I traveled a lot, but I had never taken anyone with me. Now, God had placed a dream in my heart to start leading teams around the world.

I sought counsel. I got input from people who had done similar things. I felt like I had a pretty solid grasp of what I needed to do to get things started.

I was excited. I told everyone about it. I shared how great of a tool travel would be for helping people expand their perspective. I shared all the amazing things we'd see. I even knew exactly where I'd take people. I grew up in Guatemala, so I was familiar with that area. I figured that was a good place to start. In college I took lots of classes about China. I decided to explore it for trips, as well.

But then it hit me.

I have no idea where to start finding people. How long will the trips be? How many people can I take? How do I handle all the money? Heck, how do I raise the money?

Reality check. I had a dream and a clear one-liner, but I had no idea how to start making it happen. My mind was constantly stirring with ideas, but I wasn't coming up with anything I could put into action.

When you get to this point, make sure you always keep something handy for writing the idea down. Ideas are precious, but they can easily be lost. Don't let it get away by assuming you'll remember it. Write it down!

For several weeks, I wrote myself little notes when I had ideas about how to implement the plan. The pile of little scraps of paper was getting rather high on my rickety Formica desk. I needed a central place to put all my ideas.

I had already written out my one-liner across the top of the white poster board. The rest of it was blank. Then I did what at the time seemed like common sense. Looking back, I realize that God showed me a really powerful, simple tool for getting started on any dream. It's a tool that helps take the big dream and break it down into step-by-step goals—a map to get me to where I was certain God was taking me.

I went to the very bottom of the poster board that had my one-liner boldly written across the top. Based on input from advisors, at the very bottom I wrote the first step: *Form an organization.*

That's it. That's how my Vision Map started. It's not rocket science.

The Vision Map serves two simple purposes. First, it is your Vision written out to see. Second, it goes from a broad, wide goal at the top and narrows down to very specific steps. The one-liner clarifies your vision and gives you a destination. The Vision Map is your strategy for how to get there.

The one-liner clarifies your vision and gives you a destination. The Vision Map is your strategy for how to get there.

Use the Vision Map to write out ideas that come to you. Write out strategies. Write out the names of people who could potentially help you. Brainstorm ideas off to the side.

I want to reiterate here. Don't count on your memory to hold on to good ideas! Write them down as soon as you get them. If you are away from your Vision Map and an idea comes to you, type it into your phone or scribble it on a piece of paper. Then transfer it to the Vision Map as soon as you can. If you wake up in the middle of the night with an idea, drag yourself out of bed and write it down. Don't just hope to remember it in the morning. Don't let those ideas fly away in your sleep.

Put all your ideas, thoughts, and strategies on your Vision Map so that they're all in one place. As God leads you, there's a good chance you'll begin to see connections in the ideas that could bring some amazing breakthroughs or take your dream to the next level.

So here's my advice. Run down to the store right now and get the supplies you need:

1 large poster board
1 black marker
1 red marker (I'll explain this later)

That's all you need to get started. Go grab them, and I'll finish my story when you get back.

"Write the vision; make it plain on tablets,
so he may run who reads it."

—Habakkuk 2:2

5} DIVIDE AND CONQUER

MY VISION MAP WAS beginning to take shape.

The goal was already written across the top. I even had my first step: start an organization. So I did some research. I learned that I needed to decide what kind of organization I wanted to start. A lawyer seemed my best bet for that kind of advice.

That would be my next step. As I was reaching for my black marker a grim reality slapped my optimistic face. Lawyers cost money. Lots of it. Money I didn't have.

My heart sank. I had come to the first dream dasher of a visionary—an obstacle. It was a big one. Money.

I set down the black marker. I was frustrated. So I started praying. Actually, it more resembled complaining.

"God, You gave me this big dream. You even gave me this creative way to map out a plan, but I'm already stuck on the first step! I have no money! This is going to be impossible."

I moaned and complained for a few minutes and then I

remembered something. What I was trying to do really was impossible—impossible if I was trying to do it in my strength.

I didn't have the resources or the knowledge to pull this off, but the One who gave me the dream on that mountain in Russia definitely did. He had, and still has, all the resources and knowledge in the world. Yes, He had called me to an impossible task. However, this forced me to remind myself, *"With man this is impossible, but with God all things are possible"* (Matthew 19:26).

YOUR PART, GOD'S PART

I love the story of King Jehoshaphat in 2 Chronicles 20. An enormous army came against him. He was outnumbered. Jehoshaphat was terrified and began to seek the Lord.

After some frantic prayer, God speaks to Jehoshaphat and the people. *"Thus says the Lord to you, 'Do not be afraid and do not be dismayed at this great horde, for the battle is not yours but God's . . . Tomorrow go out against them, and the Lord will be with you'"* (2 Chronicles 20:15,17).

The following day, God won the battle for Jehoshaphat without him ever having to fight. God did the impossible.

It's unlikely you'll ever have to go into a physical war for your dream, but there's a good chance you are feeling overwhelmed by the size of the challenge in front of you. When the feeling of being overwhelmed and outnumbered starts burning in your stomach, I suggest you do like Jehoshaphat: divide and conquer.

Seek counsel and figure out what is within your power to do. But remember you aren't in this alone. The dream in your heart was God's from the beginning. You are partnering with Him on the

When God gives us a vision, it's a different kind of partnership. He can do it all on His own. But He lets us in on the fun for His glory and our joy.

project. It's His dream. You just get to be part of it. It's a partnership.

When two people get together to form a partnership, it's usually because they both have something to bring to the table, a unique set of skills or financial assets that will supplement the operation. When God gives us a vision, it's a different kind of partnership. He can do it all on His own. But He lets us in on the fun for His glory and our joy.

When I got overwhelmed by the tasks in front of me, I had to take a step back. I had to remember I was called to do the possible. I'd leave the impossible to my Quiet Partner.

I knew I needed a way to determine what I could do and what only God could accomplish. So I scrounged around in the kitchen and just happened to find a red marker. I stormed back up to my room and just above the first step of *start an organization* I wrote the next step in bright red. It was something that was totally out of my control.

Find a lawyer for advice on starting an organization (for free).

With this step I also had a clear prayer focus. I knew exactly what I needed to pray for. Forget the big vision. I needed something very specific.

When you get to this point in mapping your vision, remember to take it step-by-step. Write down every step you can think of that you need to take with the black marker, even little steps that don't seem important. Write them down.

Set small goals.

Then set a deadline.

Make a reasonable timeline. We overestimate what we can do in a few weeks, but we underestimate what can be accomplished in a few months or a year.

Be realistic about your current schedule. If you are working full-time, give yourself a few months. Starting a blog? Give yourself a few weeks to think through what you want the blog to be about. Writing a book? You won't write it in a month. But you can do one chapter in a month. Making a pilot program for TV? It's going to take some time.

Nothing kills the dream quicker than setting unrealistic goals. But your small-step goals should also push you a little. They should require some faith.

Set a time frame for each step you can take. You can't put one on your red-letter goals—those are up to God. But you can set time goals for the steps that are within your control.

Don't be surprised if soon after writing down the steps you begin to see God bringing about those red-letter items. When you divide responsibility, it's amazing how quickly God begins to do His part. It may take longer than you want, but just because you don't see anything happening doesn't mean nothing is taking place. God is always working. Keep doing your part knowing God is doing His.

If you've started your Vision Map, there's a good chance you've already come to an obstacle—something only the God of the impossible can pull off. If that's the case, then you are in a great place. Remember, if you could do this without God it wouldn't be a God Idea. It would only be a good idea.

Whip out your markers and start writing out steps. Make them very specific. Read on, I'll share why.

"If God be your partner, make your plans large."

—D. L. Moody

6} PRAY, PRAY, PRAY

I ALWAYS FIND THIS story fascinating:

> *And as they went out of Jericho, a great crowd followed [Jesus]. And behold, there were two blind men sitting by the roadside, and when they heard that Jesus was passing by, they cried out, "Lord, have mercy on us, Son of David!" The crowd rebuked them, telling them to be silent, but they cried out all the more, "Lord, have mercy on us, Son of David!" And stopping, Jesus called them and said, "What do you want me to do for you?" They said to him, "Lord, let our eyes be opened." And Jesus in pity touched their eyes, and immediately they recovered their sight and followed him* (Matthew 20:29–34).

A couple of observations:

1. These guys just called out for mercy. It started out as a generic cry for help.

2. Jesus seems a little obnoxious making them spell out their need. Wasn't it obvious? The dudes were blind—of course they wanted to see!

Jesus wanted the men to be specific about their need. He required them to focus on exactly what they wanted from Him. Based on this story, it seems He wants us to express our specific needs to Him.

I think one of the most powerful results of making your own Vision Map is it forces you to get specific about what you need. When we get specific, eventually we will encounter impossible things that only God is capable of doing.

When you reach your first impossible task, a step on the Vision Map that is completely out of your power to pull off, then you are in a good place. Why? Because I'm certain that's where God wants us—driven to our knees.

Remember, this is a partnership: God, your Quiet Partner; and you. Don't ever forget that order. If God is ever in any role other than Chief Executive Officer of your vision, then you have a problem. God lets us be part of what He's doing. We have a part to play, but ultimately it all comes down to Him.

Earlier, I mentioned that no one can prepare you for all the challenges you'll face, but that's not exactly true. There is one advisor who knows all the steps. He knows exactly what you need to do. The great thing is He's also your Quiet Partner. There are some impossible tasks that will be evident from the outset. There will be others that you'll never see coming. That's why prayer is so important.

You see, the heart of prayer isn't talking or asking for stuff.

The heart of prayer is listening.

Based on the story above, I believe Jesus wants us to ask Him for specific things. But I also believe He wants us to be quiet and listen. It's a balancing act. Some folks have a hard time talking honestly with God; others find it tough to listen. Find that healthy balance of talking and listening.

Ask, listen, and then—as the blind men followed Christ after He healed them—obey what you hear God asking.

WHAT'S THE POINT?

Now, what I'm about to say could seem like I'm undermining the whole need for a Vision Map. I'm not. I still think it's a powerful tool. But it's absolutely essential that you remember to stay in constant communication with God through prayer.

Ready or not, there are going to be lots of surprises thrown at you on this journey toward the vision God gave you. Many times the Vision Map will seem completely irrelevant because God will operate so far outside the parameters of your little plans. You may get to a place where you wonder whether it's necessary even to have a plan.

God operates on His time schedule. He operates by His plans, not our Vision Map or our brilliant ideas about how things should work. He can do whatever He wants. You get that option when you are the most powerful force in the universe!

This is why prayer is so, so, so important. You need to listen to your CEO and Quiet Partner at all times. He's quiet, but He's not silent. He wants to let you in on what He's up to.

God knows where this train is going. We should always do

what we can. We should take the steps we see in front of us, but ultimately we need to check in with God all the time. Prayer is that means of communication.

If you are going to get where God is taking you, you will need to be dedicated to prayer. Those red-letter goals on your Vision Map are a great beginning. They are a tangible way to figure out specifics to pray about. Once you've gone through this part of the process, then you need to spend some time listening.

If you listen, you'll hear God's voice. You'll be in constant communication with your Quiet Partner. He may even give you insight into ways to avoid some unnecessary work.

After your regular pow-wows with God, get to work doing what you can. Remember, while you are doing your part, God is doing His. Keep your eyes open.

I started praying hard over that one red-letter request. It's all I could do. Then God moved, but I nearly missed it.

> *"Work as if everything depended on you,*
> *pray as if everything depended on God."*
>
> —Ignatius of Loyola, Theologian, Priest, Knight

7 } STAY ALERT

MY VISION MAP HAD BEEN hanging on the wall for about two weeks at this point. At the top was my big dream. At the bottom were two steps. One in black. One in red. That's as far as it had gotten.

I'd been praying that God would connect me with a lawyer who would be willing to help a punk kid with a big idea. I called a few attorneys but never heard back from them. I didn't think I knew any lawyers.

But then it happened.

I was visiting my grandpa. One day, while running errands with him, we swung by a lawyer's office. The attorney was drawing up papers for some business deal my grandpa was working on. It didn't even occur to me that God was about to do something. In truth, I was anxious to get home.

My grandpa had a hard time walking, so he asked me to run into the office and ask the lawyer to come out and talk to him. I wasn't exactly thrilled about the request, but I did it. When Mr. Andrews appeared in the doorway, I realized I knew him. He shook my hand and at that moment my mind began churning. *Could this guy help me?*

He followed me out to the car and conversed for a few minutes with my grandpa. All the while I was sitting in the passenger seat thinking how I could bring up the subject. I didn't want to be manipulative. Their conversation ended, and Mr. Andrews ducked his head down, smiling at me through the window.

"What are you up to these days, Joël?"

I got nervous. By this point, however, I had told hundreds of people my one-liner. Once I slipped into explaining my vision I became more comfortable. As the explanation was ending I got a little brave.

"Actually Mr. Andrews, I've been needing some advice from an expert on what kind of organization I should start. What do you think?"

He thought for a moment. Then he asked me a few questions.

By this time I had stepped out of the car and we were standing in the Texas summer heat. Sweat was dripping down our faces. "Well, it sounds like what you want to do is start a not-for-profit organization. It's a little complicated to do, but it offers the best protection for what you are trying to accomplish."

God can do in one moment what it would take you fifty years to do on your own.

I was elated. I thanked him for his advice and shook his hand. I jumped back into the car. God had answered my prayer for free legal consultation. I now knew what I needed to start doing. I was ecstatic for half of the drive home.

Never forget this: One touch of God's favor can change everything in an instant. God can do in one moment what it would take you fifty years to do on your own.

Looking back I tend to brush over what God did for me as a coincidence. But it really was a miracle. I was frustrated and had no idea what to do, but I prayed and I saw God come through with what seemed impossible. I just had to stay alert.

Impossible things happen every day.

I believe we should live with a sense of expectation. Faith that God is at work. When you serve an all-powerful God—the same God who put the dream in your heart—you need to be alert to what is going on around you. Pray and then believe God is going to come through. It may not look like what you had pictured. God gets really creative. So stay attentive every day to what God is doing around you.

Expect to see lots of small miracles on the path to your dream. Every time you cross off a step on your Vision Map, it will build your faith, reminding you that God is working. Visionaries need to be alert for what their Quiet Partner is doing around them. It may happen when you least expect it.

My excitement about my chance meeting with the attorney subsided halfway home. It hit me: I was still in the same situation as before.

Sure I knew what kind of organization I needed to start, but I still had no idea how to do it. On top of that the attorney had told me it was complicated. Great! I don't do complicated very well.

For the rest of the day I was in another world, researching not-for-profit organizations. It was just as Mr. Andrews had described—complicated.

My grandpa interrupted my research by asking me more questions about what I was trying to do. He liked the idea. I told him how discouraged I was at how hard it was going to be to get the organization started.

It was at that moment my grandpa suggested something so simple I almost blew him off.

"Our tendency is to pray for miracles. But in most situations, it is more appropriate to pray for opportunities."

—ANDY STANLEY, *Visioneering*

8 } MAKE A BIG ASK

"WHY DON'T YOU ASK Mr. Andrews if he'll do the paperwork and filing for you to start the organization?"

I stared at my grandpa for a moment. "I would, but doesn't he charge lots of money for that kind of stuff?"

"Sure. But ask him to do it for free."

Despite the fact that I had been praying for an attorney who would be willing to take me on for free, a bolt of fear shot through my chest. "Free?"

"Sure. The worst he'll say is no."

That simple idea reminded me of an invaluable lesson.

If you are going to do this thing God put in your heart, you need to get comfortable making Big Asks, big requests for help.

I was terrified. I was asking an attorney to help me with my crazy idea. He had no reason to help. It was no benefit to him. Before I knew what was happening, my grandpa had dialed the number. He got past the secretary and handed me the phone. My

Never say no for someone else.

hand was shaking.

"Uhm. Mr. Andrews? This is Joël."

"Hi Joël. Call me Mark, by the way."

"Uh. Okay. So, I was wondering . . . would you be willing to help me start the organization and file all the paperwork?"

With no hesitation he spoke three words that rocketed my little heart to Cloud Nine. "I'd love to!"

I gasped. "Thank you! Thank you! But . . . I don't have any money." So much for the bold request.

"I'd be happy to do it for you for free. You'll just need to cover the filing fee with the state and the IRS. I'll do all the paperwork. Just swing by and give me the details of the name and address, etc."

My whole body was shaking by now. My Quiet Partner had been at work behind the scenes doing His thing. The seemingly impossible.

I thanked Mark and hung up the phone. I relayed the information to my grandpa. He immediately offered to pay for the costs of the filing fees with the state and the IRS, without me even asking.

BAM!

Like that, we were back in business, or actually, about to be in business for the first time.

All it took was me being bold enough to make the Big Ask. (And to be honest, I wasn't even bold.)

You'll need to do the same. You'll have to overcome the fear of getting rejected. That's the hardest part. I can almost guarantee no physical harm will come from you asking. The worst they can say is no. They might say, "No, you dummy." But hey, we've been called worse names than that before, right?

Never say no for someone else.

A friend of mine had a dream to make a movie. Years before they had funding for the film, he put a picture of a well-known actor on his version of a Vision Map. He wanted that actor for a key role. Eventually they got the funding, but because this was his first movie, their budget was small. Money was tight. What this actor charged was more than their entire budget. Through a series of miracles he was able to get his script into the hands of the actor. My friend explained the financial limitations. They asked him if he'd play the role. Guess what? The actor loved the script so much he took the role at a great financial cost to him.

Too often we assume we know what someone will say and never ask. Don't be afraid to ask. You might just be floored when they say yes.

I've heard story after story of people making Big Asks and then finding their Quiet Partner has been working behind the scenes, leading to a yes.

When God gives you a dream, He'll set up the opportunities and connections you need to make it happen. God used one of His children to help the vision take a step forward. But Mark the attorney was only the beginning.

"Audentes fortuna iuuat."

—LATIN PROVERB MEANING, "Fortune favors the bold."

9} BUILD A TRIBE

A GOD IDEA ALWAYS involves people. There's no way around it. How can I make such a definitive statement? Well, it's because the One who gave you your idea is all about people. He loves them. Really loves them. Think John 3:16.

Any idea, passion, or message He gives you to share with the world is going to involve people in one way or another. People matter.

Visionaries need people. God made it that way. If you are going to make a difference, which, if you are reading this book I assume you want to do, then you need people. They will be a key ingredient. Some will be *incredibly* important in your vision.

You need a community around you. Yes, your Quiet Partner is doing His part. He doesn't need to call on human beings for assistance. You and I do. This is why you must become a leader of people.

"Wait, I'm no leader," you say?

Well, I hate to break it to you, but you are.

God has called you to be a leader of the message and vision He gave you to share with the world. It's really not as terrifying as you think it will be. You have the vision and God will bring people along. You just need to spearhead it. You need to rally people around your idea and show them how they can be part of it.

You know how excited you get when you start sharing that God Idea of yours? Well, that excitement is contagious.

Still sound scary?

It's humbling, for sure. But you can do this.

After all, there is a problem that the world needs you to solve for God's glory and everyone's joy. You know how excited you get when you start sharing that God Idea of yours? Well, that excitement is contagious.

Your excitement can spread—it can spread like a wildfire.

I was consulting with someone recently who wants to start a TV show. She has a huge vision. She was feeling overwhelmed. I reminded her that she wouldn't be able to do it on her own. Her best bet was to start sharing her vision with people who had skills she lacked. Rather than learn every technical element of making a TV program, she should focus on what she knew best and count on God to bring people who could help her where she was not as experienced. Fortunately, she works at a church that has a TV ministry. I recommended she start looking for folks she could bring on board right there at home.

Untapped talent is all around us. It's really fulfilling when you are able to help people pursue their callings, as they help you pursue your calling. It becomes a blessing to everyone involved.

Don't try to do it all on your own. Invite people to come on board with your vision. You may just find that their dreams will come true as they help you with your dream. God likes to work that way.

One of the most practical things you can do during this stage is to keep an ongoing list of things you need help with. Always be ready to immediately answer when someone asks, "How can I help you?" I meet lots of people who, when I ask them how I can help, tell me they'll have to get back to me. Don't miss an opportunity to bring someone on board. Always be ready to give folks a way they can help, right when they ask.

If you'll be bold and start sharing your vision, God will bring people into your path to be part of the tribe you are starting—a band of people who share a vision that's similar to yours. They'll love your vision, and follow you. I guarantee it.

Mr. Andrews, the attorney, was one of the first people who caught the vision for what God had placed in my heart. He wanted to help. He used his unique skills and training to help advance the vision that God had given to me. All I had to do was share it and ask.

However, one lawyer and me did not an outdoor adventure team make. I knew I needed more people. So I kept telling people—everyone I could. Then I met Brad.

Brad was so excited about the concept that he raised his own financial support to join me. He had lots of churches recruiting him to come work for them right out of college. Rather than take a stable job and salary, he raised money to be part of my vision. At his own expense, he even went with me to scout the destinations where we'd eventually take our groups.

Vision doesn't stick. It has to be re-presented over and over. Make sure everyone in your tribe constantly has the vision in front of them.

Brad got it. He understood what I was trying to accomplish, and he jumped on board with the vision. He even helped recruit several people for our first trip.

God will provide you with people who will "get it." Never take those people for granted. They are a gift from God. They will be integral in getting the word out and helping you accomplish what God has called you to do.

Sure, there will be some people who won't get on board. I write to people all the time asking if they want to be part of one of our outdoor adventure trips. They say no. There are lots of people who don't like the outdoors. They don't know what they are missing, but that's not my problem. I just have to share the vision with everyone I meet. God brings the right people into my path. He will do the same for you.

Don't take your tribe for granted. Every person matters. Those who have signed on with the vision God gave you will need to be constantly reminded of the vision. That's your job. Vision doesn't stick. It has to be re-presented over and over. Make sure everyone in your tribe constantly has the vision in front of them. Don't assume they think about your dream as much as you do. Constantly share the vision with them. Communicate. Lead them.

You have a problem to solve and a message to share with the

world. You can't do it alone. You need people. Even one person is a solid start.

> *"You will get all you want in life, if you help enough other people get what they want."*
>
> —Zig Ziglar, *Secrets of Closing the Sale*

10} START SMALL

I WAS BEGINNING TO SEE huge potential for the organization. But as my mind was exploding with the possibilities, I was also getting overwhelmed. How was I going to handle all the massive growth I was sure was just around the corner?

I was still getting counsel from lots of people. They were using words like "expand," "replicate," and "scalable model." I liked the sound of that, but it started to overwhelm me. I found myself awake at night trying to figure out how to make this thing grow bigger, faster. I hadn't technically started, but I wanted it to get huge.

It turned stressful and overwhelming rather than fun and exciting.

I remember talking to my dad about how anxious I was, trying to grow the organization. He told me something I've never forgotten in any venture I've taken on since. It's four simple words.

Start small. Grow slow.

SMALL BEGINNINGS

I was talking with a guy recently who has a dream to start a beer brewery. He was certain that he needed at least $250,000 to get started. That amount seemed insurmountable for him, so he had pretty much written off his dream as being impossible apart from some miraculous financial intervention.

"Why can't you just start with what you have?" I asked.

He gave me a perplexed look. "But I can only produce about one hundred bottles per day out of my house."

"Could you sell those one hundred bottles?"

"Easily." No hesitation from him.

"So sell those hundred, then sell a hundred more and a hundred more. Start small. Grow slow."

I saw something change in that moment. His smoldering dream flickered back into a flame.

I think one of the biggest things that holds dreamers and visionaries back is this false notion we got, from who knows where, that we have to start big.

Go big or go home! I disagree with that statement. When you start small and build slowly, you learn along the way. You get experience and knowledge you'll need when things get big. Your mistakes aren't life or death. They hurt a little, but they aren't going to level you.

Don't let your desire to have a big, perfect growth plan stop you from moving forward. General Patton once said, "A good plan violently executed now is better than a perfect plan executed next week."[2]

Nothing can kill a dream quicker than wanting perfection and planning too much. I meet so many people who have an enormous organizational structure and growth plan all worked out, but they are so set on having a massive system that they feel they can't start without huge amounts of funding or office space or a book deal.

Many of those people struggle to see their dream take off because they are bogged down by thinking too big. Don't get me wrong. I want you to dream big, but you still have to start small.

You don't need a massive infrastructure to start most things. Just start small and do it well.

You don't need a massive infrastructure to start most things. Just start small and do it well.

I love Zechariah 4:10 (NLT): *"Do not despise these small beginnings, for the Lord rejoices to see the work begin."*

God rejoices when He sees your work begin, no matter how small. Remember, your Quiet Partner is the One who gets to decide how big you get, so just do what you can with the resources you have.

My friend Kassie has a dream to start a clothing company that serves women in developing nations. She is super creative, but internal resistance has been eating her lunch. She finally decided to start small. While I was writing this chapter I got an email from her that made me smile:

> *I made a deal with myself. I have to spend at least two hours a day in my sewing room (garage). I am working on a shirt right now. I'm so excited about it. It's going to be one of those shirts that every girl will want in her closet . . .*

I have been driving into town and checking out the boutiques. I am going to keep it simple so I don't freak out. I'm working on two pieces then I'm going to take them to some of the places I'm interested in and see what happens. I'm not even worried about making them in a bunch of different sizes and all that stuff the books I have read say to do. It's just too much for me. I'm just going to make two pieces and go for it.

If no one likes them then I haven't wasted a ton of time and money and I can just wear them myself. If they like them, then I can figure out what to do then. Just taking it one day at a time. When I get frustrated I make something small so I can feel confident again. I'm not even worried about tags and labels. Just concentrating on cutting and sewing, nothing else. I'll send you a picture as soon as I get one made. It should be soon.

I can't wait to see what happens when her Quiet Partner starts blessing the dream He put in her heart. She is taking small steps. Taking time every day to move toward her dream. I'm certain if she stays at it, she is going to look back and realize just how far she has come—one step at a time. Wanna write a book? Start writing a little bit every day. Wanna restore a broken marriage? Take it day by day. You can do nearly anything if you'll start small.

Do what you can and count on God to come through and bless your small steps.

I've only seen a few instances when God created something from nothing, but I've seen extraordinary things happen when God blesses small steps of obedience.

A few years back a friend of mine was starting a cafe in Peru. He had a huge dream. My wife, Emily, and I got so excited about it that we moved to Cuzco, Peru, to help him. After months and months of being there we still didn't have a cafe. I realized his dream was so big it was overwhelming him. He didn't have the resources he needed to build what he wanted.

One day he announced that he was giving up on the cafe. I couldn't believe it. He had put in so much hard work. We were so close to being open. But my friend was exhausted. Where we were was far from where he wanted it to be.

I asked if I could step in and start the cafe. He told me to give it my best shot.

I knew we needed to start small. I got help to get the permits we needed and opened the doors as quickly as possible. We weren't ready. I didn't know anything about the restaurant business. But we focused on doing what we could, the best we could, with the resources at hand. And guess what . . . People loved the place! Money started coming in and we were able to buy equipment we needed, slowly. Eventually we handed the cafe off to a guy who really knew business and the cafe is thriving to this day. (It was just listed in the Lonely Planet Guidebook for Peru!) That cafe would never have opened had we not started small.

Whatever you are trying to do you should always keep the future in mind. But for now, focus on doing the best you can with what you have.

Once I latched on to the concept of starting small and growing slow, that's exactly what I did with my outdoor adventure teams. I focused on making each trip the best it could be—no matter how many or how few people came. I learned from every trip. The things I learned on the smaller trips prepared me for the bigger things that were to come.

Whether you have already gotten started or you feel like you are dead in the water, I encourage you to keep thinking big, but start small. Starting small is the key. Focus on what's right in front of you. Focus on those black-letter items on your Vision Map. One step at a time. Then there's that other really frightening thing . . .

"Start where you are. Use what you have. Do what you can."

—Arthur Ashe, Tennis Star

11 } TAKE A RISK

THANKS TO MR. ANDREWS, the organization was up and running legally. Thanks in large part to Brad, we even had a full team signed up for our first trip, which was now two months away. The time had come to take a step I had been dreading for months.

I had a great job. I had worked at Southwest Airlines for seven years. I was making good money. I had five weeks of paid vacation every year. I had free travel. I had a great schedule. I was set.

My plan entailed raising support to be able to focus on mission teams full time. With our first trip approaching, it was time for me to leave the security of my salaried job.

I dropped my two weeks notice off at my supervisor's office while he was gone, hoping to avoid having to explain myself. I knew he wouldn't understand what I was about to do.

A few minutes later I received a call. "Hey, Joël. I just got your letter. Uhm. Why don't you come into my office for a few minutes."

Ugh. "Okay. I'll be there in a minute." I slowly wandered to his office, trying to figure out how I was going to explain that I thought God was calling me to quit my job.

When I arrived at his office it was worse than I expected. The manager was there too. They were both looking at my letter, perplexed. They looked up when I walked in.

"Hi. Why don't you take a seat." My supervisor motioned to a chair.

The manager started. "So what are you going to do when you leave here?"

I explained.

He raised one eyebrow. "Sounds exciting. How are you going to make money?"

"Well, I'm going to ask people to support me financially."

They looked at each other. My supervisor spoke up. "Do you have people who have promised to do that yet?"

"Well, sort of, but no. Not yet really."

More confusion came over his face. "Isn't that a little risky? I don't know if you realize it, but the economy isn't so great right now. This is a pretty good job, you know."

"Yes. This is a *very* good job." I nodded. "It's been a huge blessing. But I'm pretty sure I'm supposed to do this."

He cocked his head slightly. "What makes you so sure?"

I swallowed hard. "Well, I feel like God is asking me to do this."

An awkward smile appeared on his face. "Oh . . . don't you think God would be fine with you doing it part time and keeping a stable job?"

That supervisor had great intentions. He was really concerned for me. But at the end of that conversation fear stepped in and took me on a multi-day roller-coaster ride. Doubts began to flood my mind. *Am I really supposed to do this full time? Did I actually hear from God? What if God doesn't provide?*

Over the next few days I learned something that I still haven't quite gotten used to. It's countercultural and against my nature. It was during this crisis of faith that I learned risk is a good thing.

That's not a message you'll hear from most of the people. The message we usually hear is, "hedge your bets; minimize risk." I do think that's good advice for some things, but it's bad advice when it comes to doing something that will bring God glory.

At one point in your vision, probably at multiple points, you will be required to step out and take a serious risk. Decisiveness and action will be required. The outcome of that decision or action could lead to loss. Loss of reputation. Loss of finances. In extreme cases you may even end up risking loss of life for God's glory.

That risk is godly.

God can take no risks. When you are all-knowing, all-powerful, and ever present, risk isn't even within your realm of possibilities. God controls everything. That eliminates any potential for risk.

But we *can* take risks. I'm convinced God will ask us to take risks for the sake of His glory and our joy.

I believe that one of the greatest ways we can bring glory to God with our lives is by showing the world that we hope in something different. The world goes after power, influence, and money for security. If you have one or all three of those you have control (supposedly). Many people think their hope and security come from those things.

Christ-followers are called to a different hope. We are called to show the world that our hope is always in Jesus. Regardless of how much or how little power we have, despite our degree of influence, and no matter what our finances look like, our hope is Jesus.

That's how God gets the glory. When we are willing to risk power, influence, finances, and even our lives—put them on the line for God—then we draw attention to a different way of living.

Your vision will require risk. It will require you to show the world that you place your confidence in your Quiet Partner.

In obedience to your Quiet Partner, you may have to quit a solid job. You may have to invest money that was set to guarantee you a great retirement. You may even have to put your well-being on the line. Well-meaning people will tell you that what you're doing is dangerous. Their caution doesn't guarantee that it is.

Regardless of how much or how little power we have, despite our degree of influence, and no matter what our finances look like, our hope is Jesus.

Always pray and seek counsel before you take the leap. I've seen people take unnecessary risks. It may be that God wants you to start small and keep your day job. Each situation is different and everyone's journey is unique. What God called me to required that I quit my job. What He has called you to may not require the same thing. Just make sure that you obey whatever He asks of you.

I wish I could tell you that when you take a risk it will always come out peachy. Unfortunately, I can say from first-hand experience that isn't always the case.

A good friend of mine set out to start her own business. She quit a well-paying job to pursue her dream of opening a cafe. A year after opening, she closed the business. She was disappointed, but she says she doesn't regret having tried. Too many people are left wondering what could have been. She tried, and things didn't work out like she expected—but at least she tried. Ultimately it led to her stepping out into new areas she wouldn't have had the courage for before. She ended up moving to a new city and now has an amazing job. Her seeming failure actually gave her more courage!

Sometimes God allows us to take a risk that seems to result in failure. You'll put it all on the line, and it will seem like God left you hanging.

If that happens, as long as you obeyed what He asked, don't get discouraged. God is still working. God is ALWAYS working and He doesn't waste any experience, good or bad.

Your God Idea is going to require risk.

Little did I know, the meeting with my supervisor was the beginning of two of the scariest weeks of my life. For what felt like the first time, I truly confronted the risk. But God wasn't done yet. As if quitting my job wasn't enough, I would never have believed what else He was going to ask of me.

"Be bold and mighty forces will come to your aid."

—Basil King, *The Conquest of Fear*

12 } MAKE A SACRIFICE (SORT OF)

TWO WEEKENDS BEFORE MY last day at Southwest Airlines, I had a Saturday off. A friend of mine invited me to a Bible school graduation in Dallas. I didn't know the person graduating, but I thought it'd be a fun road trip.

Had I known what was waiting for me when we got there I'm sure I wouldn't have gone.

During the commencement ceremony, the founder of the Bible school got up and said they needed to raise $20,000. She said that she felt there were twenty people in the building who God was telling to give $1,000 each.

When the words left her mouth my heart sank. I knew I was supposed to be one of those people. So I did the spiritual thing.

I ran out of the building.

My friend Jacoby followed me outside. "Are you okay?" he asked.

"Ya, I'm fine," I said, charging ahead, trying to get as far away from the building as possible. We walked in silence until we arrived at a McDonald's. I ordered a Big Mac.

Seated at a booth, my friend wouldn't back down. "Dude, I know something's bothering you. What's up?"

I sighed. "Man, I'm quitting my job in two weeks. I'm trying to raise support to go do my mission trips. I've saved $5,000. That's the most money I've ever had in my life. I could live off that for a few months I think. I might need it just in case . . . you know."

"In case what?"

I didn't dare complete my sentence. If I had completed it, I would've said, ". . . just in case God doesn't come through."

"So what's the problem?" My friend continued pushing.

"Well, I think I'm supposed to be one of the people that gives $1,000 dollars, like the founder said."

My friend let out a roaring laugh. I motioned for him to quiet down. He was drawing attention to us. "So you think that by leaving the building you'll get away from that?"

I could feel my cheeks getting red. "No, well, I mean . . . I don't know. This is just really bad timing to be giving away money. That's my backup fund."

"Dude," my friend thundered. "If God told you to give, you'd better obey. Now!"

I grunted. There were a few moments of silence as I finished my hamburger. *Why was I even in Dallas at a graduation? I should never have come.* I thought about my Vision Map. This definitely wasn't in the plans. I thought about the miracles God had done up to this point.

And then I decided. "Okay. Let's go."

We headed to the accounting office of the school and I wrote out a check for $1,000. That was the most money I had ever given away in my life. Monday morning I checked my bank account, and my security fund had gone from $5,000 to $4,000.

Then things got worse.

A few days later I received a letter from a friend who was raising support for a mission trip. As I read it I was sure God was telling me to give her $1,000.

I'll never forget the moment that I signed that check, sitting at the table in my nearly empty room, boxes all packed for my upcoming move. One lone lightbulb hung over the small oak table as I looked up, pen in hand, and said, "God, I'm doing this, but You had *better* provide for me!" I was angry and probably a bit disrespectful to my Quiet Partner, but I obeyed.

Long story short, over the next ten days God systematically dismantled my savings account. I gave almost all of it away. It was as if God was saying, "Are you really going to trust Me? Then prove it. Make a sacrifice."

Let me make something clear.

You cannot sacrifice for God.

He won't let you.

The minute you think you've sacrificed, He'll open up the floodgates and drown you in blessings you could never have imagined. God has access to everything you could ever need. Oftentimes, God releases that provision after we've taken a step of faith. You may have to let something go to make room for what's to come. He wants us to exercise our faith in Him. *"And without faith it is impossible to please him"* (Hebrews 11:6). When we obey in faith, with no guarantee of the outcome, we are glorifying God and showing our trust in Him. The results of walking in this kind of faith will often go beyond your wildest dreams.

You won't see that on the front side of obedience. It only comes after you take the risk—after you make the seeming sacrifice and obey.

THE BLESSING OF SACRIFICE

When I was twelve years old, my dad announced he was going to ruin my life.

"Your mother and I feel God is calling us to move to Guatemala, Central America."

I started crying. This was horrible news. Guatemala was a developing country in the middle of a civil war. Poverty was everywhere. There was rampant violence from insurgent guerrilla fighters. They were blowing things up, kidnapping kids, and killing innocent people. The government was also known for some questionable tactics in the war. It was hard to tell a difference between the good guys and the bad guys. This was no place to raise a family.

Yet this was where we were going.

Dad got quite a bit of backlash from people. Even some family members questioned his decision. "You are taking your family down there? That's dangerous. I find it hard to believe God would ask you to do that to your family."

Dad and mom were sure. So they took the risk and made the sacrifice. A sacrifice that seemed like it was going to cost their family dearly.

I'm so, so thankful my parents made that sacrifice. The experience of growing up in Guatemala revolutionized my future. I'm absolutely certain that many of the blessings I'm walking in today are because my parents were gutsy enough to make a risky sacrifice for the vision God placed in their hearts.

When the time comes to take a risk for your God Idea, there is a good chance God is going to ask you to do something that seems like a major sacrifice. It may not make sense.

My advice: Do it! Post-haste. Don't hesitate. In the end, you'll find it wasn't actually a sacrifice.

The seeming sacrifice God will ask will look different for each person. But whatever He asks, just obey. Your Quiet Partner is working on something big. It's even bigger than the vision He gave you. There's something larger at stake.

"Sacrifice is a part of life. It's supposed to be. It's not something to regret. It's something to aspire to."

—MITCH ALBOM, *The Five People You Meet in Heaven*

13 } BECOME YOU

FOR THE NEXT FEW YEARS, I led teams around the world. I traveled to over twenty countries—places like Guatemala, Mexico, China, Tibet, and Mongolia—and served in dozens of mission projects. God always provided. It didn't make sense on an expense sheet. I shouldn't have been able to do as much as I did on what was coming in financially. Somehow in God's economy it worked.

After leading backpacking teams around the world for several years, I took a break and went back to get a master's degree in counseling. With the new degree in hand, I set out to take the organization I had started to the next level. I was convinced it was going to be big.

I sought counsel. I prayed hard. I wrote out a slightly modified Vision Map and started talking to people. I poured thousands and thousands of dollars into advertising for my trips. I even got a friend to pitch in several thousand to help with the cost of getting the word out.

Before I went back to school, I had led multiple trips to various destinations. We'd had great success. Several of our team members even ended up going back on the mission field for longer assignments. On my first trips I had no trouble recruiting people with little to no advertising. Now that I was ramping up my efforts, I knew that young adults would be swarming to us wanting to join our team.

The total opposite happened.

We got one person.

After months and months and thousands of dollars of advertising. We. Only. Got. One. Person.

I was devastated. I felt like I had been led off a cliff. I was sure this was what God called me to do. Advisors had agreed. God had blessed me with people for previous teams with little to no effort. But now, I was working harder than ever and absolutely nothing took. It flopped.

Looking back, I now see I learned an important lesson for anyone who has a dream: God is more concerned about who you become than what you do.

Looking back, I now see I learned an important lesson for anyone who has a dream: God is more concerned about who you become than what you do.

Yes, God placed a dream in your heart.

Yes, He gave you a message to share with the world.

Yes, He gave you a problem to solve.

But remember, God could do all that on His own. He could spread the message and solve the problem without you and without me. He doesn't need us. God is more concerned about sanctifying us than about us doing something great for Him. He wants us holy. That is a process that takes some time.

"For this is the will of God, your sanctification" (1 Thessalonians 4:3).

Above all else, God wants to make you into the person you should be. How He chooses to do that is completely up to Him. He knows what we need. I rarely like His methods. Some of them seem downright cruel. They hurt.

A. W. Tozer put it this way: "It is doubtful whether God can bless a man greatly until He has hurt him deeply."[3]

God knows exactly what He is doing. He may ask you to take a risk. After you obey, you may find yourself flat on your back looking at what seems like a total failure. You may make a sacrifice that seems to set you back. You may not see any tangible good coming from it.

Your Quiet Partner is not asleep on the job. He did not abandon you. He's the One who placed the vision in you, and He's going to bring it to completion. Even more importantly—He's going to bring *you* to completion.

"And I am sure of this, that he who began a good work in you will bring it to completion at the day of Jesus Christ" (Philippians 1:6).

I DON'T LIKE THIS FEELING

Did I ever tell you about the time I successfully killed a ministry? It's not something I typically include on my resume.

Sometimes God will allow us to fail for His greater purposes. If we can accept every experience as God teaching us something, then we will ultimately grow.

Yup. Some of my dearest friends in the world handed me their ministry in Mexico that they had spent ten years of blood, sweat, and tears building. I was supposed to come in and give it new life. I came in, all confident.

Nine months later we were closing the doors and driving away.

It seemed like we had heard from God that we were supposed to close the ministry, but I still felt like a failure. Looking back I realize just how many things I learned. Two of the biggest are that some things are only supposed to be around for a season. And, we learn more through failures than successes.

Sometimes God will allow us to fail for His greater purposes. If we can accept every experience as God teaching us something, then we will ultimately grow. We win. We haven't failed; we've just learned and grown.

That's what God wants for us. He wants us to *"grow up in every way into him who is the head, into Christ . . ."* (Ephesians 4:15).

God is more concerned about who you become than what you do.

My friend Kate loves graphic design. She started studying design in college, but for various reasons wasn't able to complete the degree. She always felt insecure about not being able to finish. She eventually found a job working at a church, where she was able to use her artistic skills by doing graphic design. This was her favorite part of her job.

The church brought in new leadership and the personality of the staff changed. Lots of extroverted types came on board. Kate is a quiet, unassuming introvert. The new folks saw themselves as designers, and because they were louder in staff meetings, they ended up taking most of her work. She was pushed out of designing anything.

Eventually she ended up leaving the job. She was discouraged. She felt like she wasn't good enough or that her personality wasn't a good match for her career goals.

Shortly after leaving the job, she started an online company selling her designs. Within a few short months she was making more money at her business than she would have ever made at the church. She told me recently, "Sometimes I forget how cool it is what I'm doing now. Especially with how horrible I felt there toward the end at the church. It's really amazing how God can turn things around!"

I believe that God allowed that situation to transpire in Kate's life to force her to step out on her own into what she really loves, and most importantly to step into a deeper understanding of herself. If that difficult situation had not happened, she might have never stepped into what she is doing today. The experience was hard, but the results were amazing.

So, if things don't go exactly as planned. If things fall apart and you are feeling discouraged. If you have to deviate from your Vision Map, or even abandon it for a while, be of good cheer. It just means God is taking some time to give you personal attention. He is making you into who He wants you to be. He wants to teach you some important lessons you'll need to know for the bright future ahead of you.

"The path of the righteous is like the morning sun, shining ever brighter till the full light of day" (Proverbs 4:18 NIV).

God will bring the vision to pass. But He's more concerned about who you become in the process.

Since God gets creative, it's important that we remember to be flexible. Always.

"Therefore, my beloved, as you have always obeyed,
so now, not only as in my presence but much more in my
absence, work out your own salvation with fear and
trembling, for it is God who works in you,
both to will and to work for his good pleasure."

—PHILIPPIANS 2:12–13

14 } ADJUST THE PLAN

AFTER EVERYTHING TANKED for my reboot of the organization, I was completely discouraged. I had made a perfect, neat plan and written it all out in Vision Map form.

I prayed. I sought advice. Every step of the way, I mapped the things I could do, and the things only God could do. Nothing worked out as I planned. I knew this was something God placed in my heart. So I stuck to the vision. But I knew something needed to change.

And there were some big changes! The biggest was, I got married to a wonderful woman who began to help me pursue the new plan. It was a new ball game. Uncharted territory. It was me plus one going after this modified dream.

Don't be surprised if somewhere along the path to your vision you need to change the plan. Write the vision in permanent marker, but stick with a pencil for the plan. It's likely to change.

I've never met a successful visionary who had absolute clarity on how things would go down when they started. Things always change slightly—sometimes drastically. God's plan is the one you need to go with. Don't get discouraged if you seem to be taking a detour. It's possible God has something even bigger in store for your vision than what you first envisioned. So . . .

Be flexible. Adjust the plan.

ON TO PLAN B

In 1968, Dr. Spencer Silver was trying to invent a super-strong glue. In the process, he created a pressure-sensitive, not-so-sticky adhesive on accident—quite the opposite of his original plan. But that glue was the foundation for what turned into the invention of sticky notes. I guarantee he never saw that coming.

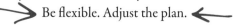

I've never met a successful visionary who had absolute clarity on how things would go down when they started.

Where would we be without sticky notes? Dr. Silver's plan change changed the world!

There's a good chance your vision won't come out exactly as you saw it in your mind. If your plan is slightly altered from what you originally envisioned, but God seems to be blessing it—go with it!

When things didn't go as planned for the relaunch of my God Idea, I nearly threw out my Vision Map. I started wondering if I completely missed God. Maybe the vision He gave me was only for a season. It sure seemed like it had more life than the small start it already had. Maybe I was wrong.

It was during this time that God started tweaking my plan.

He reminded me of an idea I had several years earlier while out with the teams. I always wondered what it would be like to bring Christian leaders along on our outdoor adventures. I had seen that hiking brought with it a lot of time for conversation and reflection.

What if I could get a speaker to come along and share with the team as we hiked? Rather than sitting in an arena or hotel conference room and listening to a presentation, what if participants could get the same inspiration while hiking with the speaker?

I took my original plan and rewrote it. I went back to my one-liner:

Take people on spiritually focused adventure trips around the world.

That hadn't changed. I had already built the organization. The vision was still the same, but now it appeared that it might look a bit different.

I faced a new challenge. How would I get those speakers to come on the trip? I drew a short line out to the side of my Vision Map and started plotting what it would take to get a speaker for this.

I wrote *Get speaker* in black. Little did I know, that wasn't a black-letter task. It was going to be a red-letter task that required God's intervention.

I started contacting well-known authors and speakers. They all sent me back the standard letter: *We've prayerfully considered your request and blah, blah, blah . . . NO.* I was discouraged. Finding a speaker for one of these wasn't going to be as easy as I thought. I'd need to depend on my Quiet Partner.

[So I rewrote it in red: *Get speaker.*
Then, I waited.]

"Semper Gumby"

—UNOFFICIAL US MARINES MOTTO

15 } BECOME A WAITER

IF YOU'VE GOTTEN THIS FAR in the book, you are probably beginning to see that getting from the initial vision God gave me on that mountain in Russia to what I'm doing today wasn't a clear-cut route. It was a journey full of divinely ordained failures, false starts, and lots of waiting.

Ah, yes. Waiting.

Probably the hardest part of it all.

Getting a one-liner requires brainwork. Getting advice involves people. Making a Vision Map is very active. Praying, if done with zeal, can be a very involved process. Making the Big Ask and taking risks is scary and thrilling. Working with people can be fun too.

But waiting. Well, waiting is boring. It is hard. It is miserable and annoying.

The thing I hate about waiting is that I'm always wondering if nothing is happening because I should be doing more. Maybe if I just talked to one more person, went to one more conference, posted one more blog, or tweeted once more.

Waiting stinks. It's one of the hardest parts for visionaries because we are people of action. We want to see forward movement. Even a little movement is enough to reignite a flickering flame in our heart.

Waiting is so passive. It's so dull.

Or is it?

After receiving numerous rejection notices for my tweaked vision, I shelved the idea. I figured it must not be God's timing. I had done what I could. So I stopped and I waited.

It was during this time that my greatest mentor and advisor (my dad) pointed something out to me. During one of my many rants about the suffering I was enduring sitting around waiting on God to come through, my dad said something that rocked my world.

"I never think of waiting as sitting around. I think of it as waiting—as in what a waiter does."

"Huh?" I said with a perplexed look.

"Do you ever see a waiter actually waiting? No, they are usually running around doing what needs to be done."

Good point. Pause. "So what does that mean for me?"

"Well, get into motion. Remember, an object in motion stays in motion."

My mind flashed back to ninth grade science class. *An object in motion . . .* Newton's Laws of Motion! We had to memorize those laws. The essence of the first law is this: An object in motion tends to stay in motion. A non-moving object tends to stay still.

We followed up on that principle by learning the difference between potential and kinetic energy. Remember those? Potential energy is stored energy. Kinetic energy is active and moving. It's being used. Put together, I'm pretty sure that these are more than just physical principles. They are also spiritual principles.

If you want God to use you—get moving.

Do something every day to move you toward your goal. No matter how small. Make a call. Send a card. Write a set number of words. Meet a new person. Go to a conference. Read a book. Take a class. Take a small step.

He'll direct you once you are in motion. If you aren't in motion, there's less chance for redirection. God likes to use the principles He put into play in His universe.

I regularly have parents who want me to talk to their young adult children. When I hear the following line, I get nervous: "My son has lots of potential. He just needs someone to inspire him."

I've come to learn that the loose translation for that statement is: "My son is a bum who is going nowhere. He needs someone to kick his butt into action."

When you reach the time when your vision seems to be stopped in its tracks, I propose you wait.

But not wait as in "sitting around on your potential."

I propose you wait like a waiter and get kinetic. Start doing something. Start serving. Just get involved with what's in front of you.

I worked with my brother at a church for a few years. He was the go-to guy for anything artsy or techy. The tech part wasn't really what he enjoyed doing most, but he was good at it, and very faithful. Every day I would walk past his office and see him working on a little website he started. It was about church stage designs. I never said anything, but I always thought it was kind of goofy. Who needs a website about church stages? But Jonathan faithfully worked on that website for several years.

Then something happened.

His website started getting upwards of 400,000 regular views. My brother became known as an expert on creativity. People asked him to speak at conferences. He did consultations for churches. Soon he shifted into being a full-time blogger. He gets more job offers than he knows what to do with. Nearly every church I visit knows about his website. Everybody wants him. All because he was faithful at his work and did what was in front of him.

God tends to use people who are doing something already. Those are the people who seem to have doors of opportunity fly open for them.

I've seen it over and over. God tends to use people who are doing something already. Those are the people who seem to have doors of opportunity fly open for them. They can be serving in an area that seems completely irrelevant to the vision God gave them and then *WHAM!* All of a sudden God places them right where they need to be for the vision to begin moving forward again.

In reality, the vision never stopped moving forward. Your Quiet Partner is working behind the scenes. In the meantime, take King Solomon's advice: *"Whatever your hand finds to do, do it with your might"* (Ecclesiastes 9:10).

I did precisely that. I started serving in our young adults group at the church. Soon I was leading the group. Then, something amazing happened.

"I waited patiently for the Lord;
he inclined to me and heard my cry."

—Psalm 40:1

16 } LISTEN FOR THE WORD "GO"

I WAS LEADING THE COLLEGE group at our church in Texas. I would have much rather been leading people on outdoor adventures around the world, but God made it clear He had a different plan for now.

The Vision Map was still on the wall in my office, but there had been no movement up toward the goal. So I waited. Actively. Serving the young adults at our church.

I took our college group to a Passion Conference in Dallas. While I was there, I ran into a friend. He told me about a book he was reading by a guy named Mark Batterson. I figured I should read it too. That night I went to my hotel room and ordered the book. Thanks to Amazon Prime, it was waiting for me when I got home.

I read the book, fast—in two days. I have a hard time getting to the end of most books, but not this one.

The morning after I reached the last page, I woke up at 4:00 a.m. I was wide awake.

I try to see only one four o'clock per day. The a.m. version is not the preferred one. When I'm wide awake at that hour, I pay attention. I sat up in bed and, clear as day, I heard God tell me: "It's time to move on the idea. Contact Mark Batterson."

I had no idea how to contact Mark Batterson. I didn't actually know that much about him. I stumbled into the guest room, fired up the computer, and whipped out an email. I gave him my one-liner and a brief explanation of my vision.

Then, I guessed at his email address.

I figured eventually the email might make its way in front of his assistant or something. Then I'd get the letter. *We've prayerfully considered your request and blah, blah, blah . . . NO.*

Having done what I could, I jumped back into bed. It was 4:30 a.m. after all.

I woke up a few hours later, made breakfast, and then wandered into the guest room. The email sitting in my inbox nearly gave me a heart attack.

Joël,
I'm all over this idea. Let's talk about what it could look like.
Mark

Turns out, the idea I proposed to Mark was something he had just added to his list of goals in the coming years. I'd written him at the perfect time.

Did I know that?

No.

Never, ever, ever forget this: One touch of God's favor can change everything in an instant.

I was just minding my own business, serving, waiting on God to do something. Then *BAM!* Just like that, in a matter of minutes, God turned NO into GO and the vision was up and running.

Never, ever, ever forget this: One touch of God's favor can change everything in an instant.

Your Quiet Partner is the most powerful force in the universe. He cannot be stopped. He does whatever He pleases whenever He pleases. When He decides it's time to move, no matter what the circumstances may look like, He won't be stopped. Regardless of where you are or how impossible things may look, God can change everything in the blink of an eye.

You just remain faithful. Years of preparation can turn into a miracle overnight. Keep your sails ready.

I'll admit it. At times I thought the vision God gave me might be dead. I thought the time might have passed. I even wondered if I had messed it up somehow—maybe I made a strategic error.

God was at work the whole time. When the time was right, through a series of seemingly random circumstances, my Quiet Partner put everything into place.

A year after I sent that email, Mark and fifteen other guys hiked the Inca Trail in Peru with me, and Summit Leaders was born. When God decides to move, you'd better be ready to go.

I went. And here we are today.

"Whatever the Lord pleases, he does,
in heaven and on earth, in the seas and all deeps."

—Psalm 135:6

17} REMEMBER

MY ORIGINAL VISION MAP got tossed somewhere in one of the many moves we've made in the last ten years, but I still have the original steps written in a little journal. I took the time to write it all down, knowing that old poster board would probably get thrown out one day. I treasure that little journal.

When the children of Israel crossed the Jordan River and entered the Promised Land after forty years of preparation, their leader Joshua asked them to do something very intentional: *"Take up twelve stones from the middle of the Jordan . . . and carry them over with you and put them down at the place where you stay tonight"* (Joshua 4:3 NIV).

He told them to take those stones and make a monument, an altar.

The altar was there *"to serve as a sign among you. In the future, when your children ask you, 'What do these stones mean?'"* (Joshua 4:6 NIV). They could go back and tell the story of God's miraculous intervention to get them into the Promised Land.

What I love about the Vision Map is that it gives you a chance to look back and see how God came through every step of the way toward your vision. It serves to remind you of God's faithfulness in the past.

Those red-letter requests that God answered are miracles. Remember them.

You may not keep the original poster board. But I encourage you to be intentional about saving meaningful things here and there that can serve as reminders of God's faithfulness on the journey to your vision. Let them serve as a reminder, a monument of remembrance. I've got the journal. I've got a hat from living in Peru. I've got pictures.

My friend Petra saw God come through in miraculous ways when her family was making a movie called *Return to the Hiding Place*. She has a watch she got at Corrie ten Boom's watch shop in Holland while filming. She made it into a necklace to remind her of God's faithfulness step-by-step as they made the movie.

You should do the same. Document God's goodness in your life.

When I feel discouraged, I go back and look at those little reminders. I can't stay discouraged for long. They remind me that God is in control and He has been with me.

Life comes at us in seasons. There will be some seasons that are more difficult than others. It's important during those difficult times to remember God's faithfulness. Go back to that monument and offer up your thanks for His goodness in the past. It's a great way to stir your faith and remember that God is still able and still working no matter how hard things may be.

Make sure you keep track of God's faithfulness. Don't let time hide the miracles He did to get you there. Remember them.

"Learn to record in writing the providences of God in your life, for by so doing you will preserve the memory of them for future meditations and encouragement."

—John Flavel, Puritan Author

18 } AND THAT'S HOW YOU DO IT

THAT'S MY STORY. That's how I stumbled and bumbled my way to where I am today.

Am I impacting millions? No. Maybe one day I will. Or maybe I won't. My Quiet Partner gets to decide that one.

Either way, the journey has taught me a lot. The vision God gave me is more about who He's making me into than what I end up doing.

The vision He gave you is the same. He placed it there. If you are patient and work hard, He'll bring it to pass. Things like the Vision Map I outlined in this book are simple things you can do to help yourself get organized. Ultimately, though, God is the One who will make it work.

When people ask me how I started doing what I'm doing, I rarely tell them this whole story. I usually say, "Just start."

It's really quite simple. Make a plan. Get moving. Start small. Use the Vision Map. Do what you can.

As you've read from my story, it's usually not a straight line. God will rarely get you from Point A to Point B of your vision via the simplest, most straightforward route.

God seems to like detours. At least that's what they seem like to us. I'm convinced it's all part of His plan. I don't think it's because He likes messing with us. I think it's because He wants to teach us that the vision He gave is more about the journey than the destination.

You'll notice I said He's taking you to Point B, not Point Z. This journey is ongoing. Even when you think you've arrived, there's more adventure ahead. Keep listening to your Quiet Partner. He's got more dreams for you.

You are His vision. He wants to make you into something great.

Get out there and change the world. Obey God. Always remember to enjoy the journey to your vision.

> *"It is good to have an end to journey toward; but it is the journey that matters, in the end."*
>
> —Ursula K. Le Guin, *The Left Hand of Darkness*

SAMPLE VISION MAPS

#1
TAKE PEOPLE ON SPIRITUALLY FOCUSED ADVENTURE AROUND THE WORLD

(My original Vision Map)

Let's do this thing!

SAFETY AND WISDOM FOR TEAM

- Create orientation program
- Buy plane tickets
- Resign from my job. Eek!!

MONEY TO BOOK PLANE TICKETS

- Set a date for the first trip

ONGOING FINANCIAL SUPPORTERS

- Talk to potential donors about the ministry
- Send out newsletters/support letters
- Raise a support team for monthly support

CONNECTIONS FOR PLACES TO SERVE ON MISSION FIELD

- Create a budget for the trip
- Take a scouting trip to team destination

MONEY FOR SCOUTING TRIP

- Create application forms and info packets

FIND SOMEONE TO DESIGN WEBSITE FOR FREE

- Create website

TEAM MEMBERS

- Recruit team members

MONEY FOR FILING FEES

- File papers with state and IRS

FIND AN ATTORNEY FOR CONSULTATION

- Start an organization

#2
BE DEBT-FREE IN THREE YEARS

- Stick to the budget
- Move to a cheaper apartment

FIND A CHEAPER APARTMENT

- Stop using credit cards
- Cut back on entertainment (cable, TV, movies)
- Lower our standard of living (until debt is paid)

GET A HIGHER-PAYING JOB

- Pay off smallest debts first

FIND A RELIABLE, REASONABLY PRICED CAR

- Sell the car I owe money on

FIND A FINANCIAL MENTOR AND ASK FOR HELP

MONEY FOR DAVE RAMSEY SEMINAR

- Go to Dave Ramsey Financial Peace Seminar
- Create a budget

#3
BE THE FIRST PERSON IN MY FAMILY TO GET A UNIVERSITY DEGREE

- Study my brains out!
- Register for classes
- Consult with an academic advisor about classes
- Create a list of questions to ask academic advisor
- Set up meeting with an academic advisor
- Find a place to live in my price range
- Compile family financial information for FAFSA
- Fill out Free Application for Federal Student Aid
- Research scholarships, set up meeting with scholarship office

GET FUNDING FOR COLLEGE

- Choose a major, get input from advisors

GET ACCEPTED TO A COLLEGE

MONEY FOR APPLICATION FEE

- Apply to colleges

MONEY TO VISIT COLLEGES

- Choose a few schools
- Get advice on good schools

NOTES

1. Eric Metaxas, *Amazing Grace: William Wilberforce and the Heroic Campaign to End Slavery* (New York: HarperCollins Publishers, 2007), 85.
2. "The Outage Expert: Process, Habits, Culture," http://www.theoutageexpert.com/a-good-plan-violently-executed-now-is-better-than-a-perfect-plan-executed-next-week-patton-2/, accessed January 31, 2014.
3. A. W. Tozer, *The Root of the Righteous* (Camp Hills, PA: Wingspread Publishers, 2007), chapter 39.

ACKNOWLEDGMENTS

THANKS TO MY AMAZING wife Emily, for being my best friend and biggest supporter.

To my parents Rick and Jana Malm, 99 percent of this book is wisdom I learned from you. Thanks for being a godly example.

Thanks to Charis and Jonathan Malm, the best siblings ever. Thanks for your support and inspiration.

Thanks to Randall, Natalie, and the entire Moody Publishers crew for believing in this book. You are people of vision who saw what could be and thought outside the box. Thank you!

To Wes Peterson, I am forever grateful for your friendship and support.

To David and Karen Nicholson, thank you for being lifelong mentors and friends.

To Kelli Standish, you have been a huge inspiration and constant encourager in this writing endeavor. Thanks for all your input and support.

To all the supporters of Summit Leaders and Emily and me over the years. Without you this book would not have been possible. And I really, really mean that!

To Mark Batterson, thanks for believing in me and supporting the call God placed on my life. You are a great friend and inspirational leader.

To Karen Ball, thank you for believing in me and having my back.

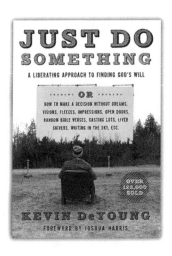

Other Moody Collective Books

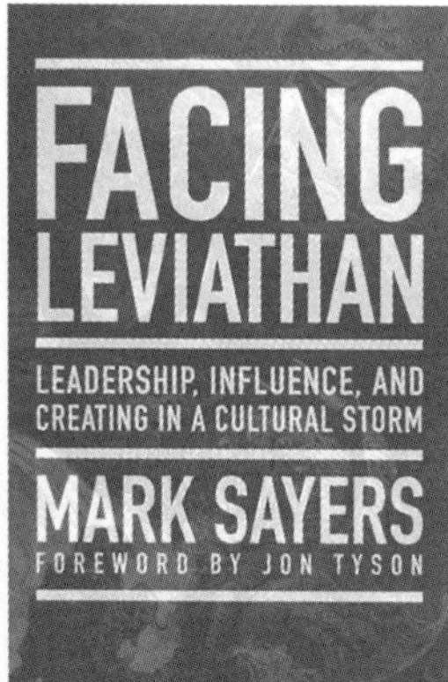

Join our email newsletter list to get resources and encouragement as you build a deeper faith.

Moody Collective brings words of life to a generation seeking deeper faith. We are a part of Moody Publishers, representing this next generation of followers of Christ through books on creativity, travel, the gospel, storytelling, decision making, leadership, and more.

We seek to know, love, and serve the millennial generation with grace and humility. Each of our books is intended to challenge and encourage our readers as they pursue God.

When you sign up for our newsletter, you'll get our emails twice a month. These will include the best of the resources we've seen online, book deals and giveaways, plus behind-the-scenes and extra content from our books and authors. Sign up at *www.moodycollective.com*.

a part of Moody Publishers

MOODYRADIO
Where you turn. For life.